Simple Thoughts and Affirmations
To Enrich Your Life

Evangeline

Simple Thoughts and Affirmations to Enrich Your Life
Copyright © 2019 by Evangeline. All rights reserved.

No part of this publication may be reproduced, stored in a retrieval system, transmitted in any way by any means, electronic, mechanical, photocopy, recording, or otherwise without the prior permission of the author except as provided by USA copyright laws.

Published by Infinite Healing 1
P.O. Box 27672, Las Vegas, Nevada 89126
Angel wings design was created by Evangeline
(graphic design by Dee Rogers)

ISBN: 978-1-941271-50-6

1. Self-help: Affirmations
2. Self-help: Spiritual
3. Self-help: Motivation & Inspirational

Printed in the USA

2 3 4 5 6 7 8 9 0

Dedication

Simple Thoughts and Affirmations to Enrich Your Life is dedicated to you, the reader. Here's to a life of enlightenment.

INTRODUCTION

When these words were originally given to me, I thought they were to be used by myself, friends, and loved ones. I have since come to understand they are to be shared with all who welcome them into their life. For in sharing these words and thoughts, I have come to realize more my divine purpose on this earth plane. I hope these words and thoughts will touch and bless you, as you continue on your life's journey. Thank you for allowing us into your life!

Acknowledgments

Thank you to all who assisted me in the journey of bringing this project to fruition and these words to print. Most of all, thank you to God, the Creator and his Energy Beings who lovingly guided me in this endeavor.

Thank you to the people who offered their inspirations and support in the roles they have played and continue to play in my life. There are those who stand out in my mind at this time whom I would like to thank.

Thank you Sonya, Ramah, Sonja, Matthew, Jorge, Robin, Lynn, Karen, Jo, and Dee. Your inspiration means more than you can imagine. May all that is good be in your life always.

To the Reader

As you head down the road of life, beware of each turn you make and recognize when you're going in circles. Stay focused so that you can maintain or even change your course if needed, for each have our own chosen path to follow.

Simple Thoughts and Affirmations
To Enrich Your Life

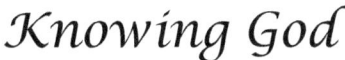

Knowing God

Thought

If you want to know more about God, learn more about yourself. This is no mystery. It is that simple. We are all a part of God, made in his image. If we come to know and understand ourselves on a deeper level, going within our being, we will better know and understand God.

Affirmation

As I come to know myself, my true being, the essence of who I am, I feel the oneness and connectedness with God the Creator. I understand that we are one. As I become one with God, I am guided to share this feeling and understanding so that all may know and enjoy this oneness.

Pure Love

Thought

The essence of who we are is pure love.

Affirmation

I am mindful of the fact that we all are the essence of pure love. I will be conscious of this whenever I encounter individuals that may annoy me. I accept that there is a lesson to be learned. With this consciousness I experience calmness and inner peace. Thank you for this con-sciousness.

Reflection

Sometimes we forget that we are the creation of pure energy/love. And the simplest acts or creatures can remind us of this with their presence or innocence. When we are reminded of our origin it is easier to accept some individuals and their contribution to the lesson being learned.

This is dedicated to Robin, my life partner, for his inspiration and to Baxter, our miniature lion, for just being.

Understanding

Thought

Understanding is more important than knowing. It is the basis of all wisdom. To simply know without understanding is incomplete. Therefore, do not take offense if asked, "Do you understand?" Perhaps it is merely a confirmation or clarification. The question should be welcomed, perhaps embraced.

Affirmation

I have an understanding of myself emotionally, mentally, spiritually, and physically of my past, and the damage this has caused my person. I am now ready to change this in a way that is most beneficial to my body, mind, emotions, and spirit. I will listen to my true self, for it knows what is best for me as I am guided through my journey.

Reflection

We may have a lot of knowledge, but if we don't understand what we know, can we fully reap the benefits? Can complete healing take place? The body exist on different levels: emotional, mental, spiritual, and physical. If any level is out of balance, illness or disease can set in. This is why it is important to have an understanding of each level of our bodies.

The Power Within

Thought

Do you know how powerful you are, how powerful each of us is?

Affirmation

I am guided to recognize and embrace the power within myself. I realize that each thought and action is powerful. Help me in focusing my thoughts and actions. I understand the healing that this process brings in all aspects of my life. Focusing and controlling my thoughts and actions is the key to personal power. And so be it. Thank you.

Creator Of My Own Reality

Thought

I am the creator of my own reality. I am responsible for my world.

Affirmation

As I awaken each day I remind myself I am the creator of my own reality. I choose to create a reality that is balanced and filled with peace, harmony, prosperity, and unconditional love. I recognize that my reality affects the universe as a whole. Thank you for this awakening.

Divine Timing

Thought

Many times we hear, things happen in divine time and we know that human time is so different. How can there be a balance between them?

Affirmation

I understand that all things have a time and place. Each of us has our own journey. I call upon the universe to align divine time with human time as I go through this process in my life. This process may now be completed with God speed and ease. Thank You!

Reflection

Sometimes we want things to happen now! Maybe now isn't the right time. Maybe we aren't ready for the lesson. We may be able to speed up the process, however the process needs to run its natural course. Asking for the alignment of time between the heavens and earth may assist in this process.

Harmony and Balance

Thought

I desire harmony and balance in my life. How can I achieve this?

Affirmation

As I awaken each day I envision my life to be balanced and harmonized. I call upon the universe to assist me in this reality. I ask that all who enter into my space this day be respectful of this energy. And so it is done. Thank you

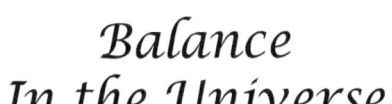

Balance In the Universe

Thought

What is balance in the universe and how do I fit in?

Affirmation

I am learning that bringing balance into the universe means giving back in some form. Showing gratitude for gifts and blessings given. As I become mindful of these gifts / blessings I feel an excitement I want to share. Thank you for these gifts / blessings and this opportunity to bring balance into the universe with my sharing.

Reflection

One may think that giving back means giving financially but that's not necessarily true. Giving back can take on many forms. Sharing one's time to volunteer or give someone in need a ride or to do a favor just because. There are many ways to bring about balance but the secret is the intent of the action. To do so with an open and loving heart. The giving itself can be the reward. Let us all give back. Let us all bring balance into the universe.

Thank you to Youri for the inspiration.

Control

Thought

Do you ever wonder why we feel the need to control when control tends to delay our progress?

Affirmation

Within my life I am aware of feeling the need to control. I now understand how unhealthy this can be, since it may interfere with ones free will or the free flow of events. I release this need and replace it with the acceptance that everyone and everything is in Divine order. Thank you for this acceptance.

This one was inspired by and is dedicated to Dee, my oldest, dearest friend. Thank you for the inspiration!

Reflection

Sometimes when we feel we are out of control in or own life we try to control other people by manipulating them, sometimes consciously, sometimes unconsciously, whether it stems from fear or insecurity. This can be unhealthy. Control certainly interferes with free will and free will is all of our rights!

Change

Thought

Do you ever find yourself thinking about what you feel needs to be changed in other people in you life?

Affirmation

As my mind tends to wonder about what I think needs to be changed in other people, I recognize the need for change within myself. I see the similarities and with this recognition I am able to make changes with ease. Thank you for this recognition.

Reflection

So many times we are quick to point out in other people characteristics that annoy us, without seeing these very same characteristics within ourselves. I believe those individuals are there to mirror changes we need to make within ourselves. Then as we change, those characteristics will no longer annoy us within others.

That Was Then, This Is Now

Thought

How do you cope when faced with present situations that remind you of past situations? Especially when the result was unpleasant?

Affirmation

When I find myself presented with situations similar to those in my past that ended with unpleasant results I remind myself, that was then and this is now! This is only a test. With that remembrance there is calmness within me. I am certain of a pleasant outcome because that was then, this is now! Thank you.

Gratitude for The Past

Thought

When you give thanks for things in your life, do you also give thanks for past situations?

Affirmation

When faced with situations of my past, I am learning to give thanks. For whatever decisions or actions I made in the past have molded who I am now and where I am in life. I like who I am and where I am. Thank you for who I am.

Reflection

When a present situation triggers memories of past situations it is for a good reason. Maybe the situation is unresolved at some level within our emotional, mental, spiritual or physical person. This is an opportunity to resolve it or an opportunity to realize and appreciate how the situation changed our life as well as to give thanks.

Going with the Flow

Thought

Do you ever feel like you keep hitting brick walls with your efforts? Like you are going against the flow?

Affirmation

I am guided to being more open every day as I continue on my journey. To go with the flow instead of against it. I am learning to recognize the signs from the universe that allows me to continue on my journey with ease, focus and understanding while fulfilling my life's purpose. Thank you for this guidance.

Reflection

When we are doing a particular job, in a relationship or any given situation where things become more challenging, perhaps it is time for a change. Instead of changing we tend to continue on the same course because the familiar feels safer than the unfamiliar. If we accept change with faith, life can become easier.

Alone Time

Thought

Ever notice how the universe sometimes puts us in a position to be alone, whether we appreciate it or not? It is precious and deserves acknowledgment.

Affirmation

I appreciate this alone time. I accomplish that which is meant to be, whether it is spiritual development, dealing with the material world, or just "being." I am never truly never alone, for we are all connected and all one. Thank you for my alone time.

Emptiness

Thought

At times, as I sit alone I have this feeling of emptiness, or of being incomplete. How can I change this?

Affirmation

I am drawn to go within myself to find and fill this feeling of emptiness. As I begin to enter the doorway of my own soul, I recognize the parts of me that have been missing or neglected. I now call them back into my person, asking God's white light to fill the space. I am now whole and complete with this reunion.

Thank you for helping me to reach completion.

Doubting

Thought

I find myself doubting myself. What is going on? How can I stop this?

Affirmation

All I have, know, and understand is within me already. I am guided to awakening this remembrance. As these memories flow through me, I am filled with confidence and certainty of who I am and my divine purpose. All is perfect in my world!

Reflection

As I become more aware of my divine purpose and myself, I have doubted at times. Am I truly this divine being, and do I truly have a divine purpose? Sometimes the answers can be overwhelming. If we ask ourselves these same questions, we need to trust the answers we receive if they resonate with us. Trust yourself.

Transition

Thought

Do you ever feel disconnected from yourself, from the God Source? Maybe you're going through a spiritual transition to a higher plane and adjusting to a new level of energy.

Affirmation

Dear God, as I am assisted during this transition, I receive your wisdom as it flows to me. I feel reconnected, balanced, and focused allowing this shift for the highest good of my being. I understand it will further the completion of my life's work on this mortal plane. Thank you.

Clutter/ Spiritual Void

Thought

What is it within my energy that makes me feel the need to hold onto that which clutters my physical space? Is it to fill a spiritual or emotional void?

Affirmation

Dear God, I am guided to remember and address the root of this issue of feeling that I need to hold onto things that cloud, clutter, and affect my entire world. Cluttering my physical space interferes with my spiritual growth. As I release my hold over this clutter, I feel a new freedom within my spiritual energy. I am becoming spiritually cleansed and complete.

Reflection

When our surroundings are filled with clutter, it hinders the free flow of energy. Therefore, does it not make sense that it will affect us spiritually, by hindering the flow of spiritual energy to and from us?

Balancing Energies

Thought

Do you ever feel as if your energy is just off or out of balance, that you just cannot focus?

Affirmation

I call into balance all of my energies- emotionally, mentally, spiritually, and physically- giving me focus, strength, and understanding. My entire being is tuned into the God-consciousness open to all of the wisdom it has to share, for all is of God.

Affirmation

I release the energy blocking me from moving forward emotionally, mentally,

spiritually, and physically, and replace it with God's white light. Emotionally, mentally, spiritually, and physically, I give myself permission to succeed. I now move forward with confidence and ease, fulfilling my destiny with clarity and strength.

Reflection

The body is comprised of four levels: emotional, mental, spiritual, and physical. When any one of these is out of balance, the body as a whole may be affected. Therefore, it is beneficial to balance all of them. Also, removing negative energies and thoughts and replacing them with positive energy or white light increases our balance and clarity.

Foreign Energies

Thought

Do you ever feel as if another energy has invaded or affected your being? Is it an individual or spirit that you cannot see?

Affirmation

As I recognize my own energies, I also recognize those that are foreign to me. They bring a feeling of uneasiness and discord. Foreign energy, if your energy is of God's white light, you are welcomed into my energy field. If it is not, I command you to leave me now. I replace that energy with God's white light. So be it.

Reflection

Sometimes when you walk into a place, you might notice a shift in your energy. If there is someone present who does not resonate with you, you might leave, but if there is not a physical being, you might feel as if a spirit entity has attached its energy to yours. Either way, you want to clear the negativity from your own energy.

Happiness

Thought

Happiness

Happiness is a state of mind. Visit it often, for you may surprise yourself with how good you feel!

Affirmation

I guide myself to find this state of happiness from within. I understand that true happiness comes from within myself. As I experience this feeling, I ask that it become contagious so that we are all in a better space. In time, may it spread throughout the world. Thank you.

Reflection

Sometimes we fell that we need someone or something in our lives to bring us happiness. While it is true that someone or something may enhance our joy, we must be happy within ourselves first; otherwise, we put the burden of our happiness on someone else. Ultimately, our lives and state of being are our own responsibility.

... *Addictions*

Thought

I recognize this addiction has a hold on me and it is time to release it.

Affirmation

I call upon the universe to bring my body, mind, and spiritto an understanding of how this addiction is affecting my entire world and those around me. I recognize that it no longer serves my purpose. I am guided to release its hold over me and replace it with God's white light, so that that I will feel renewed in love and honor.

Reflection

This can be used to assist in releasing any addiction- alcohol, drugs, overeating, even being in abusive relationships. This too can be an addiction, especially if these relationships are a constant in one's life. Releasing these things can break a cycle carried on in one's own life or in one's family.

Soulmate/ Life Partner

Thought

How do I bring my soulmate/life partner into my life?

Affirmation

I am drawn to energy of my life partner at the perfect place and time. My energy is recognized only by him/her. As our two souls connect, we are joined as one. I call upon the blessings of the universe to assist me to be in tune at this particular time. Thank you.

Reflection

Why do we sometimes need help being attuned to this? Many people do not recognize their life partners initially, which causes us not to act upon it as we should. That causes a lapse in time before that union can be recognized and acted upon as it should be.

Prosperity

Thought

How can I bring prosperity to my business and life so that I become more successful?

Affirmation

I envision my/our business (income) growing every day and bring prosperity with my vision.

My/our business (income) becomes more financially sound and grows with each passing day. I am grateful for these blessings!

My/our business (income) is an ocean with monies constantly flowing from sources known and unknown bringing prosperity to all involved. Thank you.

Reflection

I have come to recognize within my own life how positive thinking changes everything. When my business was having challenges, I realized that I needed to envision and affirm my business in a positive state instead of focusing on what was lacking.

Prosperity
Discarding Negative Energies

Thought

If you ever feel someone associated with your business is less than honest or is taking advantage of you or your business, you may wonder how you can disassociate yourself from them.

Affirmation

I call upon the universe to bring into my business only those for my soul's highest good — honest, reliable, trustworthy individuals who are pure of heart. I ask that others presently involved in my business who are not of this energy be released from my presence for the benefit of all who might be affected by their performance. Thank you. It is done. It is done. It is done.

Author's Note
Human Nature

I would like to share a little story with you and hope that it has meaning for you.

As I was finishing up writing, sitting in the park on my outstretched blanket, I looked up, realizing that I had been joined by numerous birds and wild rabbits. I took a moment to talk with them and then went back to my writing, enjoying the presence of their company. It is such a wonderful feeling connecting to nature and her creatures. Suddenly, they all disappeared, for we had been joined by a dog and its "owner." The dog took off running after the rabbits, and the birds flew off. Luckily, all the little ones found a place to hide in the bushes, trees, and air and feel safe. When the dog went back to is owner, only a couple of birds returned to visit with me. Of course, they were welcomed.

As I reflected on this, as innocent and random as it may seem on the part of the dog, I began to compare what happened with what we sometimes do unwittingly in the lives of others. Has this not happened throughout history? Hasn't man gone into another's space with little or no regard for how it affects the other? Does it still not take place even today?

If we all respect one another and each one's space, if we all accept one another and our connectedness, can we not make this earth plane a better place? Thank you for allowing me to share this with you.

All God's blessings be with you.

www.ingramcontent.com/pod-product-compliance
Lightning Source LLC
Chambersburg PA
CBHW052207110526
44591CB00012B/2109